Marshall Monroe Kirkman

The Track Accounts of Railroads and how they Should Be Kept

Marshall Monroe Kirkman

The Track Accounts of Railroads and how they Should Be Kept

ISBN/EAN: 9783744692960

Printed in Europe, USA, Canada, Australia, Japan

Cover: Foto ©ninafisch / pixelio.de

More available books at **www.hansebooks.com**

THE
TRACK ACCOUNTS

—OF—

RAILROADS

—AND—

HOW THEY SHOULD BE KEPT.

Explaining the Nature and Utility of the Roadway and Track Accounts; The Difficulties Heretofore Experienced in Keeping Them, and the Ease and Economy with which they May be Kept if Properly Arranged and Systematized; Describing How They Should be Kept, and Explaining in Detail the Information they Should Furnish and its Great Value to Railway Companies; With Detailed and Specific Instructions for the Practical Guidance of Those in Charge of the Roadway and Track, and Carefully Prepared Illustrations of the Various Forms that are Needed in Connection with the Track Returns and Accounts: Also Explaining and Illustrating the Material and Labor Accounts of the Buildings and Bridges Department.

BY

MARSHALL M. KIRKMAN.

CHICAGO:
C. N. TRIVESS, PRINTER AND ENGRAVER, 6, 8 AND 10 STATE STREET.
1882.

THE OBSTACLES TO BE OVERCOME IN INSTITUTING A TRUSTWORTHY SYSTEM OF TRACK ACCOUNTS. — ITS PRACTICABILITY. — THE UTILITY OF SUCH A SYSTEM.

One of the difficult problems in railway affairs is the institution of a system of track accounts and statistics sufficiently full to answer the requirements of careful management, that will not trespass too much upon the time of track foremen and others, and that comes within their easy comprehension Every accounting officer has experienced the difficulties of providing such a system. His labors are, moreover, too often embarrassed by the indisposition of those in charge to allow any returns of an adequate nature to be made. They do not believe such returns practicable, or are reluctant to spare the time required to make them. It is assumed in many instances that detailed accounts showing the supply and consumption of labor and material, as it actually occurs, are unnecessary. This is a mistake. No other single item of railway expense is so great as the expense of roadway and track, and it is here that the greatest care may profitably be exercised to secure favorable results. The constantly increasing necessity for economical management, renders it of vital importance that no method should be overlooked by which such results may be attained. Adequate supervision of the affairs of a corporation is impossible without carefully compiled and accurate accounts and statistics. This is especially so in regard to the roadway and track. It has long been the object of the writer, and one upon which he has experimented for many years, to institute a system of returns that would furnish the maximum of information with the minimum of labor upon the part of track men; a system that while it furnished copious information, needed only the simplest knowledge of writing and figures upon the part of those required to make the returns. This system, described in the accompanying pamphlet, has I think been practically attained. Track men of ordinary intelligence have found no difficulty in making the returns, and the information they contain has proven of great interest and value.

A comprehensive system for keeping the accounts of the material used in the track, such as the returns herein provide for, will enable the management to compare, item by item, the various articles used on different sections and on the same section in different years. This minute comparison of the quantities of material used on corresponding sections of the same line will be found highly interesting and instructive, and will be productive of valuable results to the company practising so intelligent and careful an analysis of its expenditures. It will be certain to demonstrate the difference between an economical and a profligate use of material by operatives, and so far as this is the case will prove of great value. The same particularization provided for in the case of material is repeated in the case of labor. Not only are the number of hours of work shown each day, but the object upon which this labor is expended is also stated, so that the cost in each particular instance may be ascertained and shown under its proper head. This has rendered a classification of the labor accounts necessary. The classification as contained herein has been confined to the natural divisions of track work, but it may be extended indefinitely according to the pleasure of the company interested. The minute statistical information in reference to expenditures for material and labor contemplated herein if continued over a number of years will form a valuable compendium of track expenses for the particular line they refer to, and will be conclusive of many things about which little if anything would otherwise be known. They will, moreover, afford a convenient and valuable basis for estimating the cost of track expenditures, generally, and for forming a correct judgment of the skill and economy exercised by those responsible for this important class of work.

TABLE OF CONTENTS.

CHAPTER I.

Track Accounts to be kept under the immediate supervision of Division Superintendent or Accountant. Description of the "Superintendent's Distribution of Labor Book," and "Distribution of Material Book,"with Forms and Directions for Use. Information contained in these books obtained from Labor and Material Books furnished by Track Foremen and Others. Invoices for Material forwarded to a Division to be sent to the Superintendent. Accounts with Division Superintendents kept at General Office. Track Material not charged to Operating or Construction Accounts until actually used. Provision for Securing Uniformity in Accounts between Divisions and Storehouses. What the Distribution Books returned by Division Superintendents should contain. Provision for accounting for labor expended on Material before it is Used. Accounting for Material at Rolling Mills and for Old Material. Rails Taken Up. Material Sold. - - - - 7-12

CHAPTER II.

Track Labor and the Returns made by Track Foremen. No attempt made to analyze this work upon many lines. Disadvantages suffered where this is the case. Necessity for classification of Track Labor. The Time Book to be kept by Section Foremen. Its Practicability and Simplicity. Value of the Statistics compiled from it. How the Information it contains is Compiled. Form and Directions for Use of "Section Foreman's Distribution of Track Labor." 13-19.

CHAPTER III.

Track Material and the Returns made by Track Foremen. Difficulty of obtaining Returns for such Material from this Class of Employes Why they should be Insisted Upon. Their Necessity and Value. Elaborate and Complicated Bookkeeping on the part of Section Foremen Unnecessary. Simplicity and Practicability of the Forms proposed. Forms and Directions for Use of "Section Foreman's Distribution of Track Material." - - 20-30

CHAPTER IV.

The Value of Accurate Track Returns for the Information of Managing Officers and as a Check upon Extravagance and Waste. The Records to be Kept by Division Superintendents. Material Received, Material used, Material Shipped Away or Sold, With Forms and Directions for Use. Record Books to be kept by Section Foremen. Recapitulation Book or Blank to be used by Superintendents for Distribution of Track Labor, With Form and Directions for Use. Construction Accounts. - - - - 31-37

CHAPTER V.

Inventory of Track Material, With Forms and Directions for Use. 38-40

CHAPTER VI.

The Buildings and Bridges Department, and the Labor and Material Accounts connected therewith. These accounts intimately connected with the Track Accounts. Difficulty of keeping the Labor Accounts of this Department. The kind of book required. The Information obtained therefrom Compiled by the Accountant, Provision for keeping the Material Accounts of this Department. Form and instructions for use of Distribution of Labor Book. 41-45

THE TRACK ACCOUNTS OF RAILROADS

———AND———

HOW THEY SHOULD BE KEPT.

CHAPTER I.

THE METHOD OF KEEPING TRACK ACCOUNTS EXPLAINED.

(The peculiar value that attaches to track accounts, and the necessity for their being kept in an intelligent and methodical manner, is discussed more fully in the commencement of Chapters II, III and IV than in this chapter, which is devoted largely to the details of keeping such accounts.)

The Track Accounts under the system provided for herein are kept under the immediate supervision of a division superintendent or accountant.* The superintendent or person in charge returns to the accounting officer at the close of each month two distribution books or statements, one for labor and one for material. "The Distribution of Labor book" specifies under the various headings the amounts chargeable to the several accounts on which the labor of the track force has been expended, thus:

---

* It is not material which; the idea being to have the accounts kept separately from the other material accounts by some one who can have general supervision over the work and who will be responsible to the accounting officer for the accuracy of the returns. He may be an accountant, a superintendent or a storekeeper in charge of some central depot of supply, whichever is most feasible, convenient or practicable.

"REPAIRS OF ROADWAY AND TRACK."

Name of Trackman.	No. of Section.	Time worked.	Rate.	Amount.

"The Distribution of Material" book contains a statement of the material received and from whom, the material used and on what accounts, and the material sold and shipped away and to whom. Storekeepers, including the Purchasing Agent and other supply officials, are required to charge to each division all material shipped to it during the month for use in the track; in the same manner each division is credited with the track material received from it. Track material forwarded to or received from a division is charged or credited specifically, as say, "Track Material—Central Division," the heading of the account giving the name of the division to which the material is forwarded or from which it is received. The superintendent or official in charge of the division accounts takes up in his distribution book the material that he receives and also reports the material that he has used and that he has shipped away or sold.* The several accounts upon which the material is disbursed are entered upon the distribution book by the superintendent under the proper headings in form, say, as follows:

"RENEWAL OF TIES."

Month.	Quantity and description of material.	Rate.	Amount.

The bulk of the information contained in the returns of the superintendent is obtained by him from the labor and material books made by

---

* The old material, tools and scrap that accumulate upon a division the superintendent enters as a *credit* under the head that it was originally charged to, thus old rails he credits to "Renewal of Rails" and so on.

foremen and others in charge of the track.* The "Track Foreman's Distribution of Labor Book" specifies the time worked by each man and distributes such time under the headings to which it is chargeable. The particulars of track material the superintendent obtains from the "Track Foreman's Distribution of Material Book." This latter contains the material received, used, sold and shipped away, and the material on hand as well, for each section. The information contained in these track books will be exceedingly crude and roughly written in many instances but it will be sufficiently copious and explicit to enable the superintendent to give absolutely all the track expenditures and the accounts to which such expenditures are properly chargeable. Immediately upon the receipt of the books from the various foremen the superintendent carefully examines the same and enters the aggregates in the distribution books, described above, that he sends to the accounting officer. To enable the superintendent to keep account of the track material forwarded to his division the invoices of such material are sent directly to him and it is from these that he enters his returns of material received. He in turn charges the material to the section or storehouse to which it is shipped and is thus able to hold its custodian responsible for its proper use or disposal.

At the general office a track material account is kept with each division superintendent. He is charged in this account with the amount of the track roll and with all material invoiced to him, and (incidentally) with the old material that accumulates on his division, also with all bills vouched for or approved by him on account of roadway and track. On the other hand he is credited from month to month with the total labor expended (the accounts on which it is expended being charged) and with the material and vouchers disbursed. The balance to the debit of his account on the general books should represent material, both old and new, on hand.

Such is a general outline of the method of keeping the track accounts. It conforms to the plan employed in accounting for material used in other departments, and at shops and storehouses. The details are, however, necessarily different in consequence of the lack of skill upon the part of many of those who compile the track accounts.

The details connected with the track material accounts may be stated more at length:

Track material forwarded to a division, and all expenses connected with it, including any freight charges there may be, is charged by the accounting officer directly to the division to which it is sent (never to an operating or construction account). It remains thus charged until it is

---

* These valuable books are illustrated in detail further on.

reported by the superintendent in charge as having been used, sold or shipped away. Track material should never be returned as having been used until it is actually put into the track as reported by the foremen in charge thereof.

An invoice should accompany all material. All material shipped from a division should be invoiced by the superintendent, and all material shipped to a division should be invoiced to him. Material forwarded between points on a division (where the accounts for both places are kept directly by the superintendent) should not be entered by the latter in his distribution book. All material, however, forwarded by him to other divisions or to shops or common storehouses should be invoiced and charged in the distribution books. The amount charged to a division upon the general books must correspond with the amount invoiced to such division as shown in the distribution books. In the same way the amount credited should correspond with the amount returned as disbursed. All entries on the distribution books are, however, subject to any corrections that may be necessary to make them conform to the facts in the case.

To ensure uniformity of accounts between those who forward and those who receive material (in the case of divisions, shops and common storehouses), the persons who forward and receive material should notify the persons to whom it is sent or from whom it is received on the evening of the last day of the month, of the total amount of material charged to them and received from them in the month just closed. In this way abundance of time will be given for re-examining and correcting the books, before they are sent to the accounting officer, in the event it is found that the accounts of the person forwarding material do not agree with those of the person to whom it was shipped.

Vouchers for expenses affecting the track accounts of the various divisions should be invoiced and charged to such divisions, the same as bills for material; these should be entered by the division superintendents in their distribution of material books, and charged to the proper accounts.

In the "Distribution of Material Book" required to be returned by the superintendents monthly, they will report in order as follows:

1st. All track* material received by them during the month, opening an account with each division, shop or store, from which received.

2nd. They will enter all invoices of material shipped away (including

---

*I use the word *track* throughout this pamphlet, it will be noticed, as I assume that all material that is forwarded to the shops and common storehouses of a company, including the department of buildings and bridges, is charged by the accounting officer directly to such shops, storehouses or department and that they render him distribution books for such material the same as the superintendent is required to do for track material. If, however, the superintendent is immediately and directly responsible for the material charged to either of these, (which I do not think he ever should be, as his facilities do not warrant his assuming any such responsibility), then these instructions will be understood to cover all material for which he is responsible, and for which he should account.

material sold) by them during the month, opening a separate account with each division, shop, storehouse or person to whom material is shipped or sold.

3rd. They will enter material used during the month, as reported by section foremen and others in charge of track material belonging to the division, under the head of the respective accounts upon which such material was used, as say "Renewal of Ties," "Repairs of Roadway and Track," "Construction of Side Tracks," etc.

On the last page of the book a Recapitulation of all accounts therein contained, of material received and disbursed, should be made in the order named above.

In the monthly "Distribution of Labor Book" superintendents will enter the total amount of all miscellaneous pay rolls, (including those belonging to the track,) except such as are distributed at shops and elsewhere, not included in the accounts of the superintendent. Following these entries a distribution of such rolls will be made, charging the labor performed during the month under appropriate headings to the operating or other accounts that they concern. On the last pages of the book a Recapitulation of such accounts should be made, as in the case of material. The Distribution of Material and Labor books should be sent forward on or before the 6th of the succeeding month.

The price at which material should be charged or credited, as the case may be, should be the price current at the time, or if the material has been brought forward from the last inventory, the price charged should be the same as that entered in such inventory, unless otherwise directed.

As already stated, material is not to be charged to an operating account until it is actually used. If a gang of men on, say, the Northern Division are engaged in loading ties for the Western Division, such labor should be charged to "Track Material—Western Division," and the amount should be invoiced to the superintendent of the Western Division by the superintendent of the Northern Division, the same as if it were an article of material. If a gang of men are occupied on the Central Division in loading ties for the Central Division, such labor should be charged in the "Distribution of Labor Book" of that division to "Track Material—Central Division." The amount thus entered will be charged back by the accounting officer to the Central Division, and afterwards, when the ties are used, the amount should be charged by the superintendent to the proper account in the "Distribution of Material Book."

All track material, including both old and new, at rolling and repair mills or at points off from the road should be charged to the person responsible for such material, and he should be required to make returns of the material that he receives and what disposition he has made of it in the same manner that superintendents are required to make returns.

Invoices of track material shipped to rolling mills should be forwarded to this person and should be charged under the general head of "Track Material invoiced to ———." The invoice should specify the weight of the material, or if that is not known as accurate an estimate of the same as can be made. It should, moreover, give an accurate description of the material, number and initial of car, date of shipment, number of lineal feet (in the case of rails), weight of rail per yard, etc., etc.

As already partially explained, old track material that accumulates on a division should be entered on the distribution books (in red ink) as a credit (i. e., as a deduction) at the bottom of the account to which such material was originally debited. Thus, old rails should be deducted from the amount charged in the current month to "Renewal of Rails;" but in the case of old rails one and one half per cent. should be deducted from the original weight to cover the cost of wear and tear.

In charging rails to "Renewal of Rails" the metal that is taken up should be brought (credited) on the "Distribution of Material Book" in the same month in which the charge is made. The same rule should be observed in other cases where it is applicable.

In the event labor is performed for or material sold to individuals the amount chargeable to such individuals should be entered on the distribution books as in the case of other accounts.

Under the classification of operating expenses as provided by the State Railroad Commissioners at Saratoga, the track accounts are divided under the following heads:

Repairs of Roadway and Track,
Renewal of Rails,
Renewal of Ties.

The expenditures for Bridges and Culverts are charged under the head of

Repairs of Bridges, (including Culverts and Cattle Guards.)

CHAPTER II.

TRACK LABOR—THE RETURNS MADE BY TRACK FOREMEN.

The disbursements for Track Labor form a large part of the expenses of every railroad. Upon many lines no attempt is made to specify and analyze this work. The gross amount of the wages paid to the section gangs along the line are charged in bulk to Repairs of Roadway and Track. No systematic effort is made to ascertain and compare month by month and year by year the labor expended upon the different kinds of work that engage the attention of the track force. The cost for track labor is always so great that where details are not given much difficulty is experienced in judging whether all the expenditures have been necessary or not. The same trouble is found in trying to determine the relative economy displayed upon different divisions, sub-divisions and sections of a road, and in comparing one year with another. These difficulties suggested to me that a classification of the track labor would facilitate such examinations and comparisons, and would prove valuable otherwise to those immediately responsible for the expenses connected with the roadway and track. Accordingly, some time since, I introduced the accompanying time book for use by the track force.* This book enables the foreman in charge of each section to note down at the close of each day the number of hours worked by the men under him upon the different classes of labor upon which they have been engaged. The foreman is not called on to figure the cost of the labor; simply to enter the number of hours. The Cost is determined afterwards in the office of the division accountant. Some apprehension was felt at first as to the ability

---

* For particulars of this book see instructions and illustrations of "Distribution of Track Labor," immediately following these explanations.

of the section foremen to keep these simple statistics, but after an extended experience on a road some 3,500 miles in length the system has been found to work admirably, without expense, and without the section foremen experiencing any especial difficulty in complying with all its requirements, and without diverting them from the more serious duties of looking after the roadway and track. Indeed, a man who cannot write down a few simple names or insert opposite or underneath a printed heading the number of hours worked is not fit to superintend men, or have charge of the track of a railroad, and where such men are employed and given the direction of section gangs and the care of property no great efficiency can ever be expected. Ignorance so dense is only capable of the most feeble and inconsequential advance in any direction.

The statistics that have been compiled from the information furnished by the time books in question have been found of great value to those in charge of the track, and to the managers and owners of the property. They enable the officers of a road to ascertain the relative cost each year and for a number of years of particular classes of work of great importance in the operation of railroads, such as the general repairs of roadway and track, laying ties, laying rails, ditching, freshet repairs, track watchmen, ballasting track, construction of side tracks, clearing track of snow and ice, and cutting weeds, brush and grass. This information has not only been of great value in itself but has enabled the officers in charge to exercise a minute supervision over the expenses which would not have been possible otherwise. A careful classification of track labor will enable the officers of a railroad to judge with greater accuracy from month to month as to the economy exercised by roadmasters and section foremen in the labor employed, than they would be able to exercise if they depended simply upon a comparison of the aggregate amount of the track rolls for the different divisions and sub-divisions. The information, moreover, surrounds the expense for track labor with a valuable and necessary safeguard; the necessity of specifying just what each man is engaged upon in each instance, while it does not absolutely prevent fraudulent practices, has the effect to render them more difficult by rendering them more liable of detection. In addition to the statistical information furnished by the track time book it affords the data required in making the pay-roll and it is from this source that the information required for that purpose is obtained.

In compiling the statistics, for which the track labor book affords the basis of information, the total number of hours worked upon the roadway and track proper, on each sub-division, should be footed by the superintendent. From this total the average number of men employed per mile of track may be ascertained. This average cost per mile for repairs of roadway and track is based on a full day's work for each man for the whole month. The information therefore admits of no question as to its authenticity and completeness. The track book also furnishes the data for ascertaining the cost of labor per mile of track. These statistics are of great value in making comparisons between the different divisions, sub-divisions and sections of a road, and in comparing the expenses of corresponding months in different years. Such comparisons, it may be remarked, are very interesting, and always valuable from the light they throw on the relative economy exercised upon different divisions and lines. A comparison of the number of men per mile of track for corresponding periods in different years upon the same section of track also affords a valuable and necessary check upon expenditures.

In arranging for a classification of the labor of trackmen a minute sub-division has not been attempted; the aim has been to divide the labor under the natural divisions of track work, so as to afford the management valuable information, and at the same time reduce the clerical labor to be performed by foremen to the minium. The list can be diminished or still further increased at any time as may be thought best. In addition to the track work, proper provision has also been made in the distribution of labor book for keeping account of such other classes of work as will naturally fall to the lot of trackmen, such as repairing fences, telegraph, bridges, etc.

A reference to the Distribution Book for Track Labor, as it is illustrated on the succeeding pages, with the accompanying instructions, will afford the reader a very clear insight into its form and purpose.

The "*Section Foreman's Distribution Book of Track Labor*" is as follows, viz.:—

DISTRIBUTION OF
TRACK LABOR
FOR

Section No.

*Location

FOR MONTH OF

_____188__

I hereby certify that the within is correct,

....Foreman.

Examined,

---

* The exact location of the Section must always be entered, both for Labor and Material, as, "Between Chicago and Rose Hill;" or "From one mile north of Chicago to Rose Hill; or "From one and a half miles south of Rose Hill to three miles north of Rose Hill," etc., etc. When the book is for a Train, or Gravel Pit, or Quarry, the name of same must be inserted.

INSTRUCTIONS TO TRACK FOREMEN IN REFERENCE TO

Distribution of Track Labor Book.

The total number of hours worked, should be entered in the first column headed, "Total Time Worked." Following this, Columns are provided for distributing the labor under the different headings, and track foremen are required to enter under such headings the number of hours chargeable to each as follows:

"REPAIRS OF ROADWAY AND TRACK."

General Repairs Track.—Enter the time consumed in cutting and repairing rails, repairing side tracks, taking up sidings, surfacing track and all other ordinary repairs not enumerated below.

Laying Ties.—Enter time used in taking up and disposing of old ties and unloading, handling, and laying new ties to replace those taken up.

Laying Rails.—Enter time consumed in removing and disposing of rails from track, and replacing same with other rails; also the ordinary surfacing of the track at the time the rails are laid, and loading the old rails to be sent away.

Ditching.—Enter the time used in opening, clearing, widening and perfecting ditches and drains, and cutting down or strengthening embankments.

Freshet Repairs.—Enter the time consumed in repairing damages to roadway and track caused by freshets.

Track Watchmen.—Enter time of Night Watchmen or Track Walkers.

Ballasting.—Enter work done in gravel pits, hauling gravel and stone for use in track, quarrying and breaking stone for ballast, raising and repairing track with ballast. (NOTE.—Gravel train conductors, and foremen of gravel pits, and quarries must in all cases, state on what division, sub-division and section of road the gravel or ballast is to be used, so that the expense may be properly charged.)

Clearing Track of Snow and Cutting Weeds, Brush and Grass.—This includes clearing same from the road-way and track, etc., moving and burning weeds, brush and grass inside of fences.

"REPAIRS OF FENCES, ROAD CROSSINGS AND SIGNS."

Repairing Fences, Road Crossings and Signs.—Enter time consumed in repairing and rebuilding fences, road crossings and signs.

Flagmen at Crossings.—Enter time of men engaged as flagmen at crossings.

"REPAIRS OF BRIDGES (including Culverts and Cattle Guards)."

Repairing Bridges.—Enter time consumed in repairing or strengthening bridges, culverts and cattle guards.

Bridge Watchmen.—Enter time of men engaged as bridge watchmen or bridge tenders.

"LABORERS."

Reloading Freight, Getting Cars on Track, etc.—This account includes time occupied in watching and reloading freight into cars and getting cars on the track when wrecked or disabled. It also includes time consumed in picking up lumber or other freight lost from cars along the line. (Give particulars in each case.)

Station Labor,—Enter in this column labor assisting at stations in loading and unloading freight or performing other station labor, such as attending to switches. (Give name of station in each instance and kind of work done.)

"**TELEGRAPH EXPENSES.** (**Maintenance**)", **Repairing Telegraph.**—Enter time devoted to repairing or looking after telegraph lines.

"**Construction of New Side Tracks.**"—Enter time consumed in grading and laying new side tracks and lengthening and extending old sidings.

Miscellaneous and Remarks.—Enter in this column such items or charges as do not properly belong under the headings provided, as specified above, stating in every case the nature of the work and where it was done.

The time of Track Foremen, Conductors of gravel trains, Foremen of gravel pits, should be distributed herein each day in the same manner as track laborers.

Enter the distribution of labor in this book in a plain, legible manner, at the close of each day's work and oftener when necessary. At the close of the month add up each column, and enter the footings at the bottom of the column, opposite the word "**Totals**," being careful to see that the footings of all the distribution columns (when added together) agree with the footings of the column headed "**Total Time Worked.**" The amount in dollars and cents need not be entered in the book by Foremen, but will be entered at Headquarters.

This book must be sent forward promptly, as directed, on the night of the last day of the month.

DATE.	Total Time Worked.	"REPAIRS OF ROADWAY AND TRACK."							
		General Repairs Track.	Laying Ties.	Laying Rails.	Ditching.	Freshet Repairs.	Track Watchmen.	Ballasting.	Clearing Track of snow and cutting Weeds and Grass.
1									
2									
3									
4									
5									
6									
7									
8									
9									
10									
11									
12									
13									
14									
15									
16									
17									
18									
19									
20									
21									
22									
23									
24									
25									
26									
27									
28									
29									
30									
31									
Totals.									

Sec. Foreman Do not use.

Rate, $ .... per ....

"REPAIRS OF FENCES, ETC."		"REPAIRS OF BRIDGES ETC."		"LABORERS."		Telegraph Expenses, Maintenance.	Constructing new Side Tracks.	MISCELLANEOUS AND REMARKS.
Repairing Fences, Road Crossings and Signs.	Flagmen at Crossings.	Repairing Bridges, etc.	Bridge Watchmen.	Reloading Cars, getting Cars on track, etc.	Station Labor.	Telegraph, Repairing		

CHAPTER III.

TRACK MATERIAL—THE RETURNS MADE BY TRACK FOREMEN.

One of the obstacles in the way of keeping trustworthy accounts of the track material of railroads, is the difficulty of procuring authentic returns from those immediately in charge of track material received, disbursed and on hand. When material of this kind is received on a division a large part of it is necessarily sent directly to the various section foremen. Much of this material is used in the track within a few days or weeks of its receipt, but there is necessarily quite a stock of it remaining in charge of the various foremen. In addition to the new material in store, large quantities of old material and tools accumulate. This old material is very valuable, and it is important that acurate account should so far as possible be kept of it. Indeed it is just as important to a company that accurate accounts should be kept of its material, both old and new, as it is that accurate account should be kept of the cash in the hands of the treasurer, and loss from dishonesty or neglect would not be any greater in one case than the other. An adequate system of track accounts is valuable to a railroad company for many reasons. It enables it to see that the material it buys and pays for is actually used in the track. The value of this check alone far exceeds the cost of the most elaborate system of accounts likely to ever be devised in connection with the roadway and track. In perfecting a system of track accounts it is necessary that the track foreman's return for material should contain each item of material received by him and how and when it was disbursed. It, moreover, should contain an approximate statement of the scrap and old material that has accumulated since the last return. Only Quantities need be returned by the track foreman. From these quantities the values can be determined at headquarters. The returns thus made will serve to verify the accuracy of the bills paid by the company. This information is at once a protection and a help to the purchaser. The returns, moreover, are an intimation to the track foremen that their labor is carefully and intelligently scanned, making them economical in ordering and using material, and otherwise fostering in them a higher and better appreciation of the responsibility of their position. In fact, those in charge of the track expenses, no matter who they may be, would feel under such a system that the exercise of wisdom and care on their part would not long remain unnoticed, while the inefficient and wasteful would be quickly detected. These results, so important to a railroad, cannot be secured without an adequate and correct system of track accounts. Their beneficence no one disputes, but there is a belief in the minds of a large number of people in charge of railroads that it is impracticable for foremen immediately in charge of the track, who receive and disburse the material, to make any intelligible returns of such receipts and disbursements. Superintendents are loth to ask anything except manual labor from track men. Many of them believe that the time devoted by the foremen to writing up the most simple and brief accounts can be more profitably employed in cleaning and grubbing and performing the simple duties pertaining to their place. The value of correct returns for the purpose of securing necessary and salutary checks and for the light that such returns cast upon the comparative cost of operating is overlooked or disregarded.

To secure necessary and authentic returns of material received and disbursed by track foremen it is not necessary that they should keep elaborate and complicated sets of books or make voluminous statements; the results desired can be arrived at with very little clerical work on the part of the foreman and without requiring him to possess more than an elementary knowledge of writing and figures; the records and returns of material received and disbursed by him may be so simplified that a child would have no difficulty in making them. The object that I have had before me in preparing the forms to be used by track foremen has been to make the amount of clerical work they are to perform very simple and reduce it in amount as much as possible while insisting upon their furnishing, in the rough, such data as may be required to enable the accounting officer to ascertain the nature of the material handled by them, and its value and how disposed of. These results are attained in the "Track Foreman's Distribution of Material Book," described further on. In this book track foremen and those in charge of track stores along the line are called upon to insert only the quantities, the names of the articles being printed wherever possible. Reference to the book itself, as well as to the time book they are required to keep, will show that they are of the most rudimentary and simple kind. Anyone not capable of writing up one of these books will in the majority of cases be too ignorant and stupid to have charge of property so important and valuable as that of a railroad track.

Wherever these books have been used no difficulty has been experienced, while the information they furnish has been of the greatest interest and value to the railroad company as well as the superintendents and others immediately in charge of the track.

The following is the "*Section Foreman's Distribution of Material Book*," with the instructions with reference to its use.*

---

*When there are depots of supply for track material upon a division, the persons in charge of such depot should make substantially the same reports for such material that are made by section foremen, except that instead of material used, he would naturally report material forwarded to the different sections where it is required. Track material kept with other supplies at the common storehouses of the company, when required for use, should be invoiced to the division where required, the same as if forwarded to another storehouse.

Section Foreman's
Distribution
—OF—
TRACK MATERIAL.

Section No..

....Line.

....Division.

For Month of.. 188....

....
Foreman.

☞ When this book is used for a TRAIN OR GRAVEL PIT OR QUARRY, insert name of same.

INSTRUCTIONS TO TRACK FOREMEN AND OTHERS.

This book is intended to include only the Material in the care, and under the charge of, various Section Foremen. It is not to include Fuel, or Material under the charge of Shop Clerks or Storekeepers of the Company. It will not include the material in charge of the Building and Bridge Departments, except when specially directed.

The headings of the book provide for

"**Material Received.**"
"**Material Used.**"
"**Material Shipped.**"
"**New and old Material and Tools on hand at end of month.**"

In entering and Distributing Material in this book observe the following rules, viz.:

MATERIAL RECEIVED.—(Page 1.)—Under this head enter in detail the material received during the month, in the order in which it is received.

MATERIAL USED.—(Pages 2 and 3.)—Under this head enter opposite each article, all the material of the kind described, actually used in Track during the month on account of "**Repairs of Roadway and Track,**" "**Renewal of Ties,**" or for "**Renewal of Rails.**"

Material used for other purposes such as "**Construction of New Side Tracks,**" "**Repairs of Bridges,**" (including Culverts and Cattle Guards)," "**Repairs of Buildings,**" "**Repairs of Fences, Road Crossings and Signs,**" "**Telegraph Expenses,**" (**Maintenance**), etc. etc., must be entered in the order named, using for this purpose the blank provided on page 3, for entering "Material used for other purposes." Specify opposite the articles of material thus used the name of the account upon which said material was expended: for instance should material in a Section Foreman's charge be used in repairing fences on his section he should note opposite the articles thus used "**Repairs of Fences, Road Crossings and Signs.**" If used on buildings, say, "**Repairs of Buildings,**" and so on.

When an article Used comes under the head of Old Material, or has not the same value as new material note opposite the article the word "**old,**" or give such other information as may be necessary to enable the Accounting Officer to tell what the value of the article is, or what price should be put upon it.

In entering articles of material "**Used**" during the month, enter in each case the **total** number or quantity of each kind.

Care must be taken to enter the totals opposite the names of the right article in a plain and legible manner.

CONSTRUCTION OF NEW SIDE TRACKS.—When a new Side Track is built or an old siding is extended, it must be entered under head of "Material used for other purposes." (Page 3.) State in each case where the side track is located, the length of side track that is being built, the number of feet of guard rail, also articles used and the number or quantity of same.

MATERIAL SHIPPED.—Should Material be shipped away from a Section, a record of such material must be entered on page 4 of this book, stating to whom and to what place Material was shipped, giving articles in detail, and being particular to give the amount shipped.

MATERIAL AND TOOLS ON HAND AT END OF MONTH.—Enter opposite the various articles in the proper column, the quantity on hand, so that the Accounting Officer may know the exact quantity of supplies, scrap and tools on hand on each section at the close of each month.

Foremen are required to write up this book in a **plain** and **legible** manner, and forward same as they may be directed, on the evening of the last day of the month.

MATERIAL RECEIVED BY SECTION FOREMAN.

From whom Material was Received.	CAR NO. AND INITIAL.	ARTICLES.	NUMBER OR QUANTITY.

MATERIAL USED BY SECTION FOREMAN FOR
"REPAIRS OF ROADWAY AND TRACK."
(Section Foreman must write the name of the article used when it is not printed.)

ARTICLES.	NUMBER OR QUANTITY.	ARTICLES.	NUMBER OR QUANTITY
Axes Chopping,		Lanterns, White,	
" hand,		" Red,	
Axe Helves,		" Globes,	
Adzes,		" Tubes,	
Adze Handles,			
Angle Bars,	No. of		
		Matches,	Boxes,
Brooms,			
Bolts, Sq. Nut,	Pounds,		
" Hex. Nut,	"	Nut Locks.	Number.
		Nuts,	Pounds,
Chairs, Switch,			
Crowbars,		Oil, Car,	Gallons,
Clawbars,		" Kero.	"
Cold Chisels,		" Signal	"
		Oil Cans,	
Dippers,			
Drills,		Posts, Cedar,	Number.
		" Oak,	"
		Picks,	
		Pick Handles,	
Fish Plates,	No.		
Flags, White,			
" Red,			
Frogs,		Striking Hammers,	
		Stone,	Yards.
		Spikes, R. R.,	Pounds.
		" Boat,	"
Hand Car Brasses,		" Cut,	"
Hammers,		Shovels,	"
Hand Saws,		Sledges,	"
		Sledge Handles,	
		Spike Hammers,	
		" " Handles	
		Spades,	

(CONTINUED ON PAGE 3.)

[CONTINUED FROM PAGE 2.]

MATERIAL USED BY SECTION FOREMAN FOR
"REPAIRS OF ROADWAY AND TRACK."
(Write the names of articles when they are not printed.)

ARTICLES.	NUMBER OR QUANTITY.	ARTICLES.	NUMBER OR QUANTITY.
Scythes,		**TIES** ("For Renewal of Ties.") *Used for 'Renewal of Ties.'* Oak,	
" Snaths,		Cedar,	
Scoops,		Hemlock,	
		Ash,	
		Culls,	
		Switch,	
		Bridge,	
Torpedoes,		Head Blocks,	
Tamping Bars,			
		RAILS. ("For Renewal of Rails.")	
		Steel, 60 lb.,	Feet of
		56 lb.,	"
		50 lb.,	"
Washers,	Pounds.	*Used for 'Renewal of Rails.'* Iron, 20 lb.	"
Water Kegs,		30 lb.	"
" Pails,		45 lb.	"
Waste,	Pounds,	50 lb.	"
Wheelbarrows,		54 lb.	"
Wrenches,		56 lb.	"
Wicking,		60 lb.	"
Whetstones,			

MATERIAL USED BY SECTION FOREMAN FOR OTHER PURPOSES.
(Foreman must state in every case what the material was used for.)

WHAT MATERIAL WAS USED FOR.	DESCRIPTION OF ARTICLES USED.	QUANTITY USED.

MATERIAL SHIPPED AWAY BY SECTION FOREMAN.

TO WHOM SHIPPED.	CAR NO. AND INITIAL	ARTICLES.	NUMBER OR QUANTITY

SECTION FOREMAN'S REPORT OF MATERIAL AND TOOLS ON HAND AT END OF MONTH.

(Write names of articles when they are not printed.)

ARTICLES.	QUANTITY OF New material and new tools on hand not in use.	QUANTITY OF Tools on hand in use, and old material and scrap on hand not in use.	ARTICLES.	QUANTITY OF New material and new tools on hand not in use.	QUANTITY OF Tools on hand in use and material and scrap on hand not in use.
Axes, Chopping,			Frogs, Boss,		
" Hand,			"		
Axe Helves,			Fencing, Feet		
Adzes,			" Barbed Wire, Lbs.,		
Adze Handles,			" " " Fast'ners		
Augers,			" " " Tight'rs.		
Auger Handles,			Fence Boards,		
Anvils,			Files,		
Angle Bars, No. of					
			Gauges,		
Boring Tools,			Grindstones,		
Brooms,					
Buck Saws,					
Braces and Bits,			Hand Cars,		
Board Rules,			" " Wheels.		
Brands,			" " Axles,		
Brick,			" " Handles,		
Bellows,			" " Brasses.		
Bridge Wrenches,			" " Chains,		
Bolts, Sq. Nut, Pounds.			Hammers,		
" Hex. Nuts, "			Hatchets,		
Brush Hooks,			Hand Saws,		
Cant Hooks,			Hinges,		
Chairs, Single Switch,			Hoes,		
" Double, "					
" Step,			Iron, Pounds,		
Chain, Pounds					
Crowbars,					
Claw Bars,			Jack Screws,		
Cross-cut Saws,					
Cold Chisels,					
Clamps,			Lining Bars,		
Cement, Bags,			Levels,		
Castings, Pounds			Leveling Rods,		
Chisels,			Lanterns, White,		
Crossing Signs,			" Red,		
" " Posts,			" Globes,		
Chalk,			" Tubes,		
Car Links,			Locks, Chest,		
" Pins,			" Padlocks,		
			Lumber, Oak, Feet,		
Dippers,			" Pine, "		
Drills,					
Draw Knives,			Marking Pots,		
Dump Cars,			" Brushes,		
Fish Plates, No.			Mile Posts,		
Flags, White,			Monkey Wrenches,		
" Red,					
Forges,			Nails, Pounds,		
Frogs, Crossing,			Nut Locks, Number,		

(CONTINUED ON PAGE 6.)

(CONTINUED FROM PAGE 5.)

SECTION FOREMAN'S REPORT OF MATERIAL AND TOOLS ON HAND AT END OF MONTH.

(Write the names of Articles when they are not printed.)

ARTICLES.	QUANTITY OF		ARTICLES.	QUANTITY OF	
	New material and new tools on hand not in use.	Tools on hand in use, and old material and scrap on hand not in use.		New material and new tools on hand not in use.	Tools on hand in use, and old material and scrap on hand not in use.
Nuts, Pounds	•		Sledge Handles,		
Nippers,			Spike Hammers,		
			" " Handles,		
Oil, Car, Gallons,			Spades,		
" Kero. "			Scythes,		
" Signal, "			" Snaths,		
Oil Cans,			Scrapers,		
			Scoops,		
Pinch Bars,			Screws, Dozen.		
Pike Poles,					
Paint Brushes,			Tape Lines,		
" Pots,			Tongs,		
"			Timber Trucks,		
Pumps,			Torpedoes,		
Posts, Cedar, Number,			Tamping Bars,		
" Oak, "			Tool Boxes,		
Picks,					
Pick Handles,			Vises,		
Post Augers,			Velocipedes,		
Punches,					
Piles, Feet,			Washers, Pounds,		
Pitchforks,			Water Kegs,		
			" Pails,		
Raising Bars			Waste, Pounds,		
Rail Forks,			Wheelbarrows,		
Rakes,			Wrenches,		
Ratchet Drills, '			Wicking,		
Rivets, Pounds,			Wire,		
Rollers			Whetstones,		
Rope, · Pounds,					
			TIES. (on hand not in use.)		
Screens,			Oak,		
Striking Hammers,			Cedar,		
Shears,			Ash,		
Squares,			Culls,		
Stone, Yards,			Switch,		
" Hammers,			Bridge,		
Switches, Single,			Head Blocks,		
" Double,					
" Frames,					
" Rods,			**RAILS.** (on hand not in use)		
" Lamps.			Steel. 60 lb., Feet		
Switch Houses,			56 lb., "		
" Ropes,			50 lb., "		
Spikes, R. R., Pounds,			Iron, 45 lb., Feet		
" Boat, "			50 lb., "		
" Cut, "			56 lb., "		
Shovels,			60 lb., "		
Straightening Machine,					
Spot Boards,					
Sledges.					

CHAPTER IV.

THE VALUE OF ACCURATE TRACK RETURNS.—SOME OF THE RECORDS THAT MUST BE KEPT BY THE SUPERINTENDENTS AND TRACK FOREMEN.

The foregoing pages explain and illustrate the kind of returns required for track and material and labor. These returns place in the hands of every company data for an intelligent examination of all the details connected with the expense of operating its roadway and track. This expense it may be said is equal to twenty per cent of the total cost of operating. The management may, if it chooses, ascertain from the returns thus made every article of material used and the quantity thereof and the exact cost; the number of spades and the cost thereof, the number of axes, the pounds of spike, and so on, through the thousand and one articles of material used in connection with the track. The quantity as thus ascertained will be accurate, and therefore reliable, and in so far as this is the case it will be a great advance over the present methods. It is the custom in many instances at present to charge material to the track when it is bought or when it is taken out of the general storehouses. This practice has been necessary in the early history of railroads, in consequence of a want of knowledge of how the track accounts should be kept so as to simplify the work, or partly on that account and partly in consequence of the lack of clerical facility on the part of those immediately in charge of the track. The consequence has been that the accounts thus kept never displayed the articles of material used, *prima facie*, but told in the aggregate how much material had been paid for. A great difference. To be sure, it is presumable that every thing that is paid for is received, but there should be some means of demonstrating this important and valuable fact. The articles purchased, under such methods of accounting, are never compared with the articles consumed. This we should in the case of money consider a startling omission. If we were to assume that everything that the cashier paid out was right, without exercising any surveillance over the nature of his disbursements, it would be exactly on a par with the method of keeping track accounts enforced to-day by a great many railroad companies. Large purchases are made, but whether these purchases correspond with the material used no one ever takes the trouble to ascertain, or if they do it is in a spasmodic and incomplete manner. When material is charged to track at the time of purchase no intelligent account it is apparent can be taken of the immense quantity of material on hand along the line of the road. The practice of comparing the amount consumed with the amount paid for, or in other words of requiring a rigid return of every article used, enforces responsibility, and a very necessary and important responsibility and one that no corporation can afford to neglect.

It is the same in many respects in regard to labor as it is with material. Aggregates are not sufficient; we must have the details. The circumstantiality of the account of wages due each man must be such as to lend probability to its truthfulness. It must have the "ear marks" of an authentic statement. In the same way that we must know the articles of material that are used we must know the number of hours worked by each man, and what he has been doing day by day, whether repairing bridges, or track, or fences, or telegraph, or cutting weeds, or burning grass, or whatever it may be. The necessity of giving these explanations in detail in each instance has a tendency to prevent carelessness, inattention and irregular practices upon the part of those directly and immediately responsible. If nothing were required from track foremen and others but a report of the gross time worked by themselves and the men under them each month, they would without doubt in many instances neglect to keep the details of the actual number of hours worked each day. They would in such cases write up the accounts in bulk at the end of the month, with little if any reference in many cases to the actual time that the men had been employed. The very insignificance of the work, and the little importance attached to it apparently at headquarters, would lead to or suggest such a course. The necessity of keeping the details of the time worked, and the constant inspection of these details by his superiors throughout the month, compel the person in charge to keep his record posted each day, and he is thus estopped in a measure from neglect or improper practices of any kind.

RECORD BOOKS OF TRACK MATERIAL.

The kind of returns required by the accounting officer from the superintendent or person in charge of the track accounts has been explained. They comprise a statement or book showing the receipts and disbursements of material and the amount of labor and upon what expended, and are embraced in what are known as the Distribution of Material Book and the Distribution of Labor Book. These returns are compiled in the office of the superintendent from invoices, statements and vouchers passing through his hands and from the distribution books rendered him by track foremen. The records that must necessarily be kept in the office of the superintendent have not been explained. They are exceedingly simple, being sufficient only to enable him to keep himself advised of the material and labor accounts for which he must make returns. In connection with material he must in the first place keep a

SUPERINTENDENT'S RECORD OF MATERIAL RECEIVED BY............
DIVISION, FOR................18.....*

Date of Invoice.	Where from.	Name of Storehouse or Number of Section to which Material is sent by Superintendent	Description of Articles.	Number or Quantity.	Rate.	Amount.

This book is not only a record of material received, but tells moreover the name of the track foremen or storehouse to which the material is sent by the superintendent. It not only states in detail the material chargeable to a division but it gives the disposition of the same. Every species of track material received by the superintendent, whether forwarded directly to a section or kept in depots for track supplies is entered. All vouchers and bills for expenses affecting the track account are also entered in this book. A record is thus preserved by the superintendent, in consecutive form, of everything chargeable to his account. The particulars of material forwarded to the various sections and storehouses as entered in this book should afterwards be compared with the report of material received by section foremen, and any discrepancies inquired into and adjusted.

The next record in order required by the superintendent in connection with his track accounts is a book for recapitulating the articles of material reported by section foremen as having been used in the track, so that he (the superintendent), may be able to report to the accounting officer the agregate number or quantity of the different articles used. It would be a great waste of time for him to figure each section foreman's

---

* Upon receipt of an invoice of material by a superintendent he should in turn at once invoice it to the section foreman or track storehouse to which he has it shipped. There should be no delay upon the part of the superintendent in signing and returning invoices received by him.

book by itself or attempt to ascertain the cost of each axe used, or each spade or shovel. For the purpose of simplifying his work he will desire to ascertain how many axes or spades or shovels have been used on the whole division, and when he has ascertained this he will figure the cost on the agregate, not on each particular axe or spade. This process he repeats with each article of material used by him. Some kind of a record is therefore necessary in which he may group the different articles together so as to get at the total of each. This facility he has in the

SUPERINTENDENT'S RECORD OF TRACK MATERIAL USED ON........
............DIVISION FOR.................18......

Number of Section.	LIST OF ARTICLES.										
	Axes.	Angle Bars.	Brooms	Crow- bars.	Dippers						

Having ascertained the number or quantity of each kind of articles used, the value thereof should be inserted in the record book directly below. These quantities and values should afterwards be entered in the distribution of material book, which the superintendent furnishes to the accounting officer, thus placing within the reach of the latter every detail of information known to the superintendent, or necessary to determine the number or quantity of particular articles used and the value thereof for any month or year or series of years.

A BOOK SIMILAR IN FORM TO THE FOREGOING "RECORD OF MATERIAL USED," SHOULD BE KEPT BY THE ACCOUNTING OFFICER for the purpose of ascertaining the number or quantity of each article of material sent to the division superintendent, so that the amount paid for and sent to the latter may be compared from time to time with the amount that he reports as having been actually used in the track or being still on hand. In other words, to make the system of track accounts perfect, the articles that are purchased must be checked, item by item, with the articles that are used and on hand, and they should in every instance practically agree. The book required for compiling this information may be called

THE RECORD OF ARTICLES PURCHASED AND FORWARDED TO THE VARIOUS DIVISIONS.

Not only is it necessary that the accounting officer should keep track of the number or quantity of each article sent to the superintendent, to see that it agrees with the number and quantity that the latter accounts for, but the superintendent should in the same manner see that the number or quantity of articles that he sends to the various section foremen and storehouses agrees actually with the number or quantity that they disburse.

Still another book is required by the superintendent in which to enter the material shipped away or sold by him. This book will be but little used, and may therefore be very simple in its plan. It is as follows:

SUPERINTENDENT'S RECORD OF MATERIAL SHIPPED AWAY OR SOLD ON................DIVISION FOR................18.....

Date.	To whom Shipped or To whom Sold.	Description of Articles.	Quantity.	Rate.	Amount.

SECTION FOREMAN'S RECORD BOOKS.

Not only is it essential that the superintendent should preserve a record of the material for which he is responsible, but it is also essential that the various section foremen should preserve similar records. But as the quantity that passes the hands of any one foreman is exceedingly small, the labor of bookkeeping will be correspondingly small. A common blotter or day book properly ruled with printed headings is all that is required for this purpose. It should specify in the case of material received the date of receipt, number and initial of car, from whom, description of articles and the number or quantity thereof; in the case of material used it should give the date, articles used, the number or quantity, and for what purpose;* in the case of articles shipped away or sold, the date, to whom, description of articles, the number or quantity, and number and initial of car. A book similar to this must be kept by storekeepers for track supplies, foremen of gravel pits and conductors of working trains.

To enable the Superintendent to consolidate the distribution of track labor books, as returned by track foremen, for the purpose of ascertaining the aggregate cost for each kind of labor on the division and several sub-divisions, a recapitulation book or blank is necessary, in the same way that a blank is necessary to recapitulate the articles of material purchased and used. This form, in addition to giving the cost of the different classes of work, and the total cost, must also give the number of hours worked by trackmen on the various divisions and sub-divisions, for the purpose of ascertaining the average number of men employed exclusively on track work per mile of road, and for other necessary and valuable purposes. The labor for the various sections of the different sub-divisions should be entered in their order, and each sub-division footed separately.

The following blank will serve to illustrate the kind of form required for this purpose.

SUPERINTENDENT'S RECAPITULATION OF TRACK LABOR ON......... ....DIVISION FOR................18......

Actual Number of Hours worked by Trackmen.†	Section and Sub-Division.	Number of Miles of Track.	Number of Men employed per Mile of Track.	Total Cost.	Average cost per mile of Track.	Cost of General Repairs, Roadway and Track.	Cost Laying Ties.	And so on.

*A simple tablet, or tally list, with the names of the different articles of material printed thereon may be used with advantage by section foremen, for the purpose of recapitulating the articles, or, in other words for the purpose of enabling them to arrive at the total number or quantity of each article used for entry in their distribution of material book. This tablet is also valuable to them in compiling the monthly statement of material on hand.

† Exclude time of men engaged in repairing Fences, Bridges, Telegraph and other work not strictly appertaining to Roadway and Track. For the purpose of comparing the averages for track work on different divisions and sub-divisions it should also exclude Bridge watchmen and Flagmen at crossings.

CONSTRUCTION.

The instructions contained in the Track Foreman's Labor and Material Books provide only for repairs and renewals connected with the roadway and track and for the construction of side tracks. In building a new line or in the extension of a line already in operation construction accounts should be opened under which the cost of the new line or extension should be charged. The construction accounts immediately connected with roadway and track may be summarized as follows: " Ballasting," " Bridges and Culverts," "Clearing and Grubbing," "Docks and Appurtenances thereunto belonging," " Engineering, " Fences," " Grading," "Masonry," " Miscellaneous Track Material," " Riprapping," ' Surfacing Track and Ditching," " Telegraph," " Ties," " Track Laying," " Track Rails," " Tunnels " and " Viaducts."

CHAPTER V.

INVENTORY OF TRACK MATERIAL.

An Inventory of Track Material on hand should be rendered by the Superintendents of the various divisions at the close of each half year and oftener when required. In forwarding the particulars of the inventory to the Accounting Officer, which should be done on or before the 10th of the succeeding month, the material should be classified under the general heads of "Miscellaneous Track Material," "Ties" and "Rails." The data required in making this Inventory will be found in the "Track Foreman's Distribution of Material Book" under the head of "Material and Tools on hand." The articles must be given separately and the quantity, rate and value of each inserted opposite, thus:

INVENTORY OF MATERIAL ON HAND................18....UNDER THE
CHARGE OF_____.

Articles.	Quantity.	Rate.	Value.

The inventory must not include any material or tools actually in use in the track. It should embrace all track material, both old and new on hand, including scrap and such old tools and other property not in use as may have a marketable value. It should include all ties, iron, timber, posts, and similar material belonging to the Company on the lines of the various divisions, whether such material is to be used on the division where stored or is intended for shipment.

It should not embrace fuel, or other material in charge of general storekeepers at the shops or common storehouses of the Company; such material should be reported directly to the accounting officer by the officials in charge.

The material and labor accounts of the local rail mills on the line of the road kept by the storekeepers at such points, should be included in their returns.

Ties on hand at the various depots of supply must be taken up in the inventories of the Superintendents upon whose divisions, or in the immediate vicinity of whose divisions, they are located (unless otherwise directed), except in those cases where they are in charge of the common storekeepers of the Company at shops and elsewhere.

Track material belonging to the Company at rolling mills, or en route to rolling mills, will be included in the inventory returned by the Purchasing Agent or person in whose charge such material may be.

Worn out tools and similar material having a marketable value should be entered under the general head of "scrap," but, as already stated, no material or tools in use, should be included in the inventory.

When the actual weight of scrap and similar material, including rails, is not known, a careful estimate of the same must be made. The value placed upon material appearing in the inventory is to be the price current at the time of taking such inventory, and when this is not known, information should be sought of the proper officer.

The amount of the inventory is credited to the account of the official making it, closing the account to the date for which the inventory is rendered, and brought forward to his debit for the following month.

Upon completion of the inventory of track material by the Superintendent, he will cause a balance sheet of such material to be made in his office for the half year just closed. This sheet should include the Receipts and Expenditures of track material, including vouchers, since the date of the last inventory and should state the balance; or to explain more fully, the Superintendent will charge himself with the gross amount of the last inventory, and with such material as he may have received since that time, including the old material that has accumulated; upon the other side of the account he will take credit for the gross amount of material that has been used and shipped away or sold as per his "Distribution of Material Book" rendered from month to month; the difference between these debits and credits represents the balance standing on the books of the Company to the debit of the division. If the balance harmonizes with the inventory that has just been taken by the Superintendent, no further action is required by him, but if it differs in any way from the amount of such inventory, then he must increase or diminish the amount of his charge for track material used during the month just closed by the exact amount of such difference.

The effect of such addition or deduction in his "Distribution of Material Book" for the current month, will be to make the general books of the Company balance, as they should, with the amount of the track material inventory just taken. If desired this adjustment may be made monthly by the Superintendent, so as to keep his accounts always in harmony with the facts, as based on the statement of material on hand each month as returned by the track foreman.

In adding to, or deducting from, the charge to "*Renewal of Rails*," "*Renewal of Ties*" "*Repairs of Roadway and Track*" or other accounts, so as to make the amount of material on hand, as shown by the inventory, harmonize with the balance sheet of track material described above, the difference must be added to or deducted from the account properly subject to correction. Thus if there is an excess or deficit in *Ties* the correction should be made in the "*Renewal of Ties*" account, to harmonize such excess or deficit; or if the excess or deficit is in material chargeable under the head of "*Repairs of Roadway and Track*," the Superintendent will adjust the same by adding to or deducting from the charge for the current month to "*Repairs of Roadway and Track*," and so on.

For the purpose of adjusting the general books of the Company, only the aggregate quantities (for each article) and amounts therefor of track material on hand as shown by the inventory, are required by the Accounting Officer, but so far as the accounts of the Superintendent are concerned, the latter should not only see that the aggregate amount of his inventory balances with the general books, but it is desirable that he should balance each item or article of track material, in detail. Thus the number of Axes on hand as per the inventory should be the balance remaining after charging the number brought over from previous inventory, with all additions since that time, less the number used, shipped away and sold. Other articles should be treated in the same way.

CHAPTER VI.

THE BUILDINGS AND BRIDGES DEPARTMENT, AND THE LABOR AND MATERIAL, BOOKS AND ACCOUNTS CONNECTED THEREWITH.

This department upon our railroads usually has charge of the buildings, bridges, culverts and fences. Its accounts are, therefore, intimately associated with and in some respects a part of the track accounts of a railroad. The difficulty of keeping the labor accounts of the buildings and bridges department is very great, in consequence of the fact that the men engaged in this branch of the service are widely separated and are constantly moving from one place to another, and are frequently engaged upon different work each day throughout the month. Hence in keeping account of their labor, it is necessary that the time-book should adapt itself especially to the miscellaneous character of the work upon which they are engaged. The object, therefore is to provide a book that will enable them to insert the number of hours worked and the place and kind of work; a book, moreover that can be carried in the pocket, so that the records may be written up by the workman or foreman at the close of each day. In writing up this book (as it has been arranged) the employes of the buildings and bridges department are only required to insert the rough data, or bare facts, such as the number of hours worked, where worked and kind of work. At the close of the month the book is sent to the accountant, and from it he makes the pay roll, after ascertaining the amount of wages due each employe. He also computes the cost of the various things upon which the employe has been engaged. The information that this book furnishes, enables the accounting officer to determine at his leisure the amount of labor expended upon any particular building or bridge or culvert or fence, (as the name of the structure upon which labor is performed or material used must be given in each case) and he is thus put in possession of the facts necessary to enable him to analyze with the utmost care the cost of the labor of the buildings and bridges department, and he may, if he chooses, lay before the management the expenses of keeping up the structures that we have named, or the amount expended upon any new structures or any addition, enlargement or improvement. The time book if filed away is all the record that need be preserved in the accountant's office, except the pay roll. When any details are required it is accessible, and all the statistical information in connection with the buildings and bridges department may be thus kept without expense or inconvenience.

It will be necessary in the majority of instances to keep the material accounts of the buildings and bridges department at a central office, but foremen and others should be provided with memorandum books in which they may insert the material used by them in various structures upon which they are engaged. This memorandum book will afford the accountant in charge the data he requires for determining the account of material consumed upon each structure and the cost thereof. The returns rendered the accounting officer for material received and disbursed by the buildings and bridges department, and the inventories of material on hand, should be the same as those made by other departments.

Whenever a charge is made against or a credit in favor of any particular structure its name or location should be given so that the total amount expended upon it may be ascertained at any time if desired or the total expense upon the whole road subdivided so as to show the amount expended upon each structure.

The following are the instructions for the guidance of employes connected with the buildings and bridges department that should accompany the "DISTRIBUTION OF LABOR BOOK" used by them. The form of book used is also given.

INSTRUCTIONS TO
EMPLOYES BUILDINGS AND BRIDGES DEPARTMENT.

In entering and distributing labor in time book, you will be governed by the following rules, viz.:

1. TOTAL TIME WORKED.—Insert in this column the total time worked each day, and enter the same in the proper distribution column opposite.

2. LOCATION, NAME AND DESCRIPTION.—In this column you will, in all cases, write a description of the work and carry into the proper distribution column opposite the time worked.

3. BUILDINGS.—If the labor to be distributed is expended upon buildings, you will enter under the head of "Description," the location and character of the building, as "Janesville Passenger Depot," "Racine Passenger and Freight Depot," "Freeport Shop," or "Cedar Rapids Coal House," carrying out the time worked opposite into one of the columns provided for "Repairs" "Rebuilding," or "Construction," as the case may require. The time expended in ordinary or trifling repairs of buildings should be properly entered in one of the columns headed "Repairs." The time expended in putting up a building in place of an old building worn out or destroyed, or a building that is being almost wholly rebuilt, you will enter under the head of "Rebuilding." All buildings put up where no buildings of a similar character before existed, and all extensions and enlargements of old buildings, should be charged under the head of "Construction," but in entering description, etc., of buildings being extended or enlarged and charged to "construction" you will be particular always to designate them as "Extended" or "Enlarged," as "Extending Chicago Freight Depot," or "Enlarging Milwaukee Shop."

4. BRIDGES.—For the purpose of locating the work done upon either a Bridge or Culvert, it will be sufficient to designate it by its number or name; if it has no number then designate it by the section upon which it is located and for this purpose, the distance from any Station (or Station depot, where there is one), to the nearest succeeding Station, will constitute a Section. The bridge furthest east or south upon any section will be lettered "A," the next "B," and so on to the next section. The Culvert furthest east or south upon any Section will be "No 1," the next "No. 2," and so on consecutively to the next Section. Therefore, if you are at work, upon a Bridge, you will designate it by its letter and name if it have one, otherwise by the Section, as, if you were at work upon the bridge across the Des Plaines river between Harlem and Cottage Hill Stations, you will designate it "A Des Plaines, Harlem and Cottage Hill," carrying out the time into the column for repairs or rebuilding as required. If the labor is expended upon a culvert you will designate it by its number and section, as, "No. 3, Cedar Rapids and Fairfax.

5. FENCES, ROAD-CROSSINGS AND SIGNS.—In all cases give name of place or Section, and state whether the time is expended upon a fence, gate, or crossing. Everything must be charged in column headed repairs, except in case where you are building an entirely new fence, gate, or crossing where none has before existed, or are extending or enlarging an old one; in such cases the time should be entered in the construction column.

6. MISCELLANEOUS COLUMN.—In this column enter all labor that should not properly be charged under any of the other headings, giving a clear and concise explanation of the same.

7. Employes are required to write up this book in a plain, legible manner, at the close of each day's work and oftener when necessary. At the close of the month the accountant will add up each column, and enter the footings of each column in the proper place at the bottom, opposite the word "Totals," being careful to see that the footings of all the distribution columns added across agree with the footings of the column headed "total time worked." The amount or cost, in dollars and cents will be entered by the accountant.

8. This book must be sent forward promptly, as directed, at the end of the month.

(SEE NEXT PAGE.)

BUILDINGS AND BRIDGES DEPARTMENT.—Daily Report of Labor performed in the

Occupation..

Date.	Total Time Worked.	LOCATION, NAME AND DESCRIPTION OF OBJECT UPON WHICH WORK IS DONE.	Repairs of Buildings.	Rebuilding Buildings.
1				
2				
3				
4				
5				
6				
7				
8				
9				
10				
11				
12				
13				
14				
15				
16				
17				
18				
19				
20				
21				
22				
23				
24				
25				
26				
27				
28				
29				
30				
31				
		TOTALS,		

(SEE PRECEDING PAGE.)
Month of .... 188 , By ....

Rate, $............................ per ....

Construct'n Buildings.	Reps. Brg's. (incl. Clvts. and Cattle (Guards.)	Rebldg. Brgs. (incl. Clvts. and Cattle (Guards.)	Reps. Fncs. Road Crossings and Signs.	Constn. Fncs. Road Crossings and Signs.	MISCELLANEOUS.	Date.
						1
						2
						3
						4
						5
						6
						7
						8
						9
						10
						11
						12
						13
						14
						15
						16
						17
						18
						19
						20
						21
						22
						23
						24
						25
						26
						27
						28
						29
						30
						31

www.ingramcontent.com/pod-product-compliance
Lightning Source LLC
Chambersburg PA
CBHW030709110426
42739CB00031B/1517